START WITH A VISION
HOW LEADERS ENVISION A BETTER
FUTURE AND
SHOW OTHERS HOW TO GET THERE

Ash Seddeek
Twitter @ashseddeek
ash@ashseddeek.com

Also available in print on Amazon
There is also a workbook available for Kindle and you can order copies
of it for your team members to fill out in a facilitated workshop format

Table of Contents

EXECUTIVE COACHING 6-MONTH PROGRAM

12 1/1 COACHING CALLS (2 PER MONTHS) + 1 VIP DAY

LEADERSHIP SUMMIT/RETREAT

PRIVATE LEADERSHIP RETREAT 2.5 DAYS:

Reader's Notes

This page is blank intentionally.

It's for you to jot down your current understanding of what a vision is and how it's developed. It will help you understand what your baseline understanding is right now in preparation for your reading:

ABOUT THE AUTHOR

Ash Seddeek

Favorite Quote: Our deepest fear is not that we are inadequate. Our deepest fear is that we are powerful beyond measure... as we let our own light shine, we unconsciously give other people permission to do the same."

— *Marianne Williamson,* A Return to Love: Reflections on the Principles of "A Course in Miracles"

Ash Seddeek is a business success and leadership coach, speaker and author. Ash has worked for fortune 500 companies such as Deloitte Consulting, Kaiser Permanente, Oracle, BroadVision, and Cisco Systems on leadership development, strategic account manager sales training and strategic content for large scale corporate communications experiences such as Cisco Global Sales Experience and the Partner Summit with combined 25000 annual attendees. Ash is also the author of the upcoming book: MEANING: How Leaders Create Meaning and Clarity during Times of Crisis and Opportunity. To learn about the Massive Value Program business and leadership programs, please visit ashseddeek.com to schedule your free strategy call.

You may also call or email as well: ash@ashseddeek.com
9167537432

Join the massive value conversation on Facebook

WHAT'S IN THIS E-BOOK?

In the next few pages, you will find a tool designed to walk you and your management team through the vision development process. Before this two-part tool, you will find an introductory overview of what a vision is and the vision development process.

Why Leaders Need to Start with a Vision

Leaders should start with a vision because it gives them as well as everyone in the organization a concrete visual of what the future will look like. Anything short of a detailed vision statement will leave a lot of room for misinterpretation and confusion. This is not to say that developing a vision is easy; it isn't. It is going to require a lot of work by any leader at any level.

But once you understand how to create a vision, it will start being the catalyst for a lot of change and also the source of inspiration for you and everyone else. And it will become the anchor for many of your organization's activities: branding, marketing, sales, partner and customer acquisition.

A vision gives you answers to many questions you'll always get as a leader and sometimes constantly and the more visual and detailed your vision is the less these questions will hound you. Once you provide a clear vision of the future, you will have answered questions such as:

- What are the key business priorities in the next 3-5 years?
- Why are these priorities and not others?
- How are we going to go about achieving them?
- Are these priorities driven by customer and partner input?

- When will the business achieve it priorities?
- Who will be involved and how?
- And many more valid questions from your internal and external stakeholders.

You'll find out from the vision development process steps that you end up answering these key questions and more. You'll also end up having a statement that answers three fundamental questions: once we achieve the vision,

How will we **feel?**	The vision statement will address the emotions people will experience in the event the vision becomes a reality
What will we **know?** And	The vision statement will talk about the signs and the news and the accolades the organization will get and everyone (customers, partners, the market, and employees) will find out about it.
What will we **think?** And	The vision statement will educate how we want to view the organization and its accomplishments and its position in the marketplace: our brand and what it conjures up in our minds and others' minds.
What will we **do?**	The vision statement will educate our moves, initiatives, key projects and activities. We have a very clear idea of what

	we need to create

The Vision Development Process Tool

Part One covers the vision elements required for creating positive change.

Part Two covers the strategies, systems and structures required to execute the change vision. The questions and ideas in these two parts are not meant to be exhaustive at all but rather to help you brainstorm ideas for vision development.

This process becomes more enriching once you involve others in the vision identification and formulation stages.

WHO SHOULD READ THIS?

Chief Executive Officers (CEOs), managing directors, general managers, board of directors' members, executives, government officials and practically anyone who is in a leadership and managerial position should read this vision development process tool. If you want to learn how you can increase your company's net income and shareholder value, read on.

This e-book provides you with a solid process for developing an inspiring and challenging vision for your organization, department or work-groups.

An organizational vision helps organization leaders inspire their employees and rally them around strategic long-term goals and objectives rather than their being limited by tactical and operational activities and measures. Tactical and operational activities and measures are important only as far as they support a strategic direction and a vision that everyone aspires to!

AN INTRODUCTORY OVERVIEW OF VISION DEVELOPMENT

Today's business environment poses daunting challenges for business leaders and managers regardless of what country they operate in. Today's business leaders face aggressive market- and customer-driven expectations. Their businesses have to perform successfully and produce results that deliver value for customers, suppliers and stockholders. Business leaders have to not only lead and manage their organizations on a daily basis but also, and to a considerable measure, have a clear picture of what the future of their organization is going to look like.

WHY DO YOU NEED A VISION FOR YOUR TEAM, DEPARTMENT, OR ORGANIZATION?

A vision:

- Inspires the masses and pulls them towards a common future
- Communicates direction clearly
- Guides strategy and implementation
- Provides a higher goal from the day-to-day operation

How Does A Vision Help Your Company?

A vision:

- Enhances a wide range of performance measures
- Promotes change
- Provides the basis for a strategic plan
- Motivates individuals and facilitates the recruitment of talent
- Helps keep decision-making in context

When Do You Need A Vision?

- When the direction is not clear
- When you can't articulate the value-add for what you're doing now
- When your troops are disintegrated
- When the goals are not clear
- When everyone is drawing a different painting of the future!

VISION EXAMPLES:

Example of a vision statement from Northrop Grumman

Our Vision

Our vision is to be the most trusted provider of systems and technologies that ensure the security and freedom of our nation and its allies. As the technology leader, we will define the future of defense—from undersea to outer space, and in cyberspace.

We will —

Conduct ourselves with integrity and live our Company Values

Deliver superior program performance

Foster an internal environment of innovation, collaboration, and trust

In so doing, Northrop Grumman will become our customers' partner of choice, our industry's employer of choice, and our shareholders' investment of choice.

http://www.northropgrumman.com/CorporateResponsibility/Ethics/Pages/OurVisionValuesAndBehaviors.aspx

THE NEED FOR A VISION:

Communicating a clear picture or vision of what the future should look like to employees, and stockholders is very essential for everyone's understanding of what direction the company is going. Without such a statement of direction, business managers will not necessarily know if their business unit plans map to an overall business direction. And stakeholders will not have a solid basis for their continued investment in a particular company.

Definition of Vision

So what is a vision? How does an organizational leader develop one? Let's start by defining what a "vision" is. A vision is an inspiring and rallying statement of direction and a description of a desired future state for an organization.

Vision Defined:

_____

"A vision must **focus on the future and serve as a concrete foundation for the organization.** Unlike goals and objectives, a vision does not fluctuate from year to year but serves as an enduring promise. A successful vision paints a vivid picture for the organization…A vision must give people the feeling that their lives and work are intertwined and moving toward recognizable, legitimate goals"

Source: Mark Lipton (1996) Demystifying the Development of an organizational vision. - Sloan Management Review

An organizational leader needs to articulate a vision statement that describes its attributes to others in terms of:

What will you/they see?

What will you/they hear?

How will you/they feel?

How valuable is this going to be for everyone concerned?

Let's address each one of these questions:

What will you/they see?

To answer this question, an organizational leader needs to determine what signs, accomplishments, establishments or other observable events that will be integral to the desired future state.

What will you/they hear?

To answer this question, an organizational leader needs to think of what comments and conversations will take place. Will employees hear customers make favorable comments about how satisfied they are with their company's services and products? Will outsiders such as analysts and stockholders make favorable recommendations based on great earnings and increases in market share, for example.

How will you/they feel?

To answer this question, an organizational leader needs to describe the desired future state or 'vision' in terms of how he and others are going to feel. Will there be a feeling of happiness and a sense of excitement and accomplishment or not?

How valuable is this going to be for everyone concerned?

To answer this question, an organizational leader needs to describe the desired future in terms of the impact and the result of realizing the vision he is describing. In this description, the leader will explain to each party concerned the value of this exciting future to each one of them. This will in essence provide each one with personal reasons to make sure the vision become a reality.

Example of a vision statement from The Coca Cola Company

Our Vision: Our vision serves as the framework for our Roadmap and guides every aspect of our business by describing what we need to accomplish in order to continue achieving sustainable, quality growth.

- **People:** Be a great place to work where people are inspired to be the best they can be.

- **Portfolio:** Bring to the world a portfolio of quality beverage brands that anticipate and satisfy people's desires and needs.

- **Partners:** Nurture a winning network of customers and suppliers, together we create mutual, enduring value.

- **Planet:** Be a responsible citizen that makes a difference by helping build and support sustainable communities.

- **Profit:** Maximize long-term return to shareowners while being mindful of our overall responsibilities.

- **Productivity:** Be a highly effective, lean and fast-moving organization.

http://www.coca-colacompany.com/our-company/mission-vision-values

https://www.wellsfargo.com/invest_relations/vision_values/3

Reader's Notes

_____
_____
_____
_____
_____
_____
_____
_____
_____
_____
_____
_____
_____

HOW DOES A LEADER DEVELOP HIS/HER VISION?

Although many believe that organizational leaders are either born-visionaries or not, we believe that provided a solid process and some of the guidelines presented here, today's business managers can develop an inspiring and well-grounded vision for the future.

The next chart shows a four-step process for building an organizational vision.

The Vision development Process

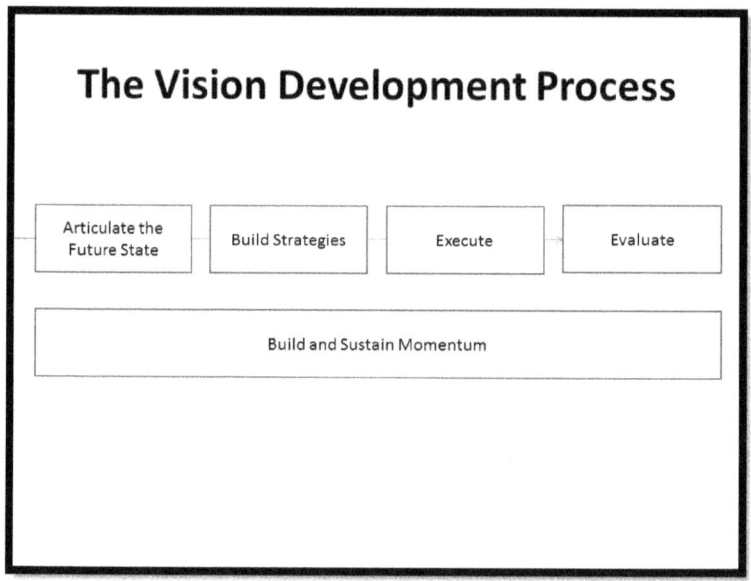

The Vision Development Process

| Articulate the Future State | Build Strategies | Execute | Evaluate |

| Build and Sustain Momentum |

THE VISION DEVELOPMENT PROCESS

Step 1: Articulate The Future State:

To articulate the future state, a business leader needs to first assess the past, present and future external and internal business environment. In his assessment, he will be able to identify how the business has measured up against goals and objectives and against its industry competitors (local and global) and against the expectations of its customers, suppliers and other stakeholders. He will also need to identify the current organizational culture, its values and the fundamental reason for its existence. Bases on such an assessment, he should be able to formulate his initial thoughts on where the business should go and how it should get there.

A business leader can at this stage start to validate his findings and thoughts for the future with other business associates and advisors. Once the initial thoughts of the desired future or 'vision' are validated and agreed on by the majority of the management team, and stakeholders such as main stockholders, an organizational leader is ready to communicate it to the rest of the organization and continue to build momentum and buy-in going forward.

Step 2: Build Strategies

Once the vision is communicated, the second step of 'building strategies' is initiated by the organizational leader and the management team. The focus of this step is on how the organization and its members will get to the desired future state; and what plans, initiatives, programs and projects will be executed to get there.

Step 3: Execute

This step is about the execution of the above-mentioned strategies, plans, initiatives and programs.

Step 4: Evaluate

This step is about constantly evaluating how all initiatives and programs are executed based on agreed-upon objectives and success metrics.

The evaluation should be iterative and constructive.

Build & Sustain Momentum

This is not a step because it is an activity a business leader wants to do at all stages of vision development, strategy formulation and execution.

Building and sustaining momentum is very important for vision realization. One of the oft-quoted reasons for the failure of organizational efforts is the lack of support, commitment, momentum and a sense of urgency.

Example of a vision statement from The Ecolab

Our Vision

Our vision keeps us focused on what we strive for – to be
the global leader in water, hygiene and energy
technologies and services; providing and protecting what
is vital: clean water, safe food, abundant energy and
healthy environments.

http://www.ecolab.com/about/our-vision

For More Vision Statement Examples: here are a couple of
websites

http://www.skills2lead.com/sample-vision-
statements.html

http://www.excellerate.com/articles/how-to-write-a-
church-vision-statement/

THE IMPORTANCE OF VALUES FOR AN ORGANIZATIONAL VISION

Vision Defined:

_____

"A meaningful vision charts a future path
that is based on a well-defined mission
…purpose, and a clear set of values"

*Source: The Art of Framing: managing the
language of leadership.*
Fairhurst & Sarr 1996

Values such as

- Excellent customer service
- Creativity and innovation
- Diversity

play a very significant role in supporting an organizational vision. Based on a 1996 Harvard Business Review article entitled Building Your Company's Vision by Collins and Porras, an organizational vision statement should include not only a description of the envisioned future but also the core ideology of a company represented in its core values and purpose.

Articulating a Vision: Components

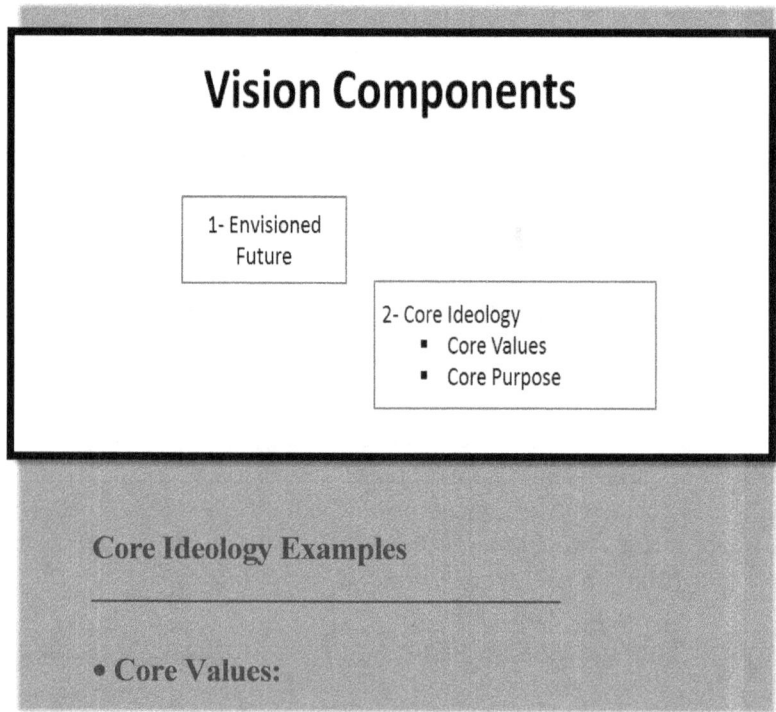

Core Ideology Examples

- **Core Values:**

- **Merck:** Corporate Social Responsibility

- **3M:** Creativity and imagination

• **Core Purpose:**

- **Merck:** To Preserve and improve human life

- **3M:** To solve unsolved problems innovatively

Collins and Porras argue that an envisioned future statement "consists of two parts: a 10-to-30 year audacious goal plus vivid descriptions of what it will be like to achieve the goal. On the one hand, it conveys concreteness-something visible, vivid and real. On the other hand, it involves a time yet unrealized-with its dreams, hopes and operations. Here are two examples of statements from two companies:

Example of an envisioned future

Our Vision:

Envisioned Future Example (1)

Charles Schwab & Co., Inc.

"Going forward, we intend to make investing easier and more accessible for more people by serving them in a variety of ways,...In the years ahead, we will serve more customers in more ways by reaching out to such groups as international investor, 401k plan participants, and institutional investors..."

Source: Adapted from the Charles Schwab Corporation Annual Report...1997

Envisioned Future Example (2)

Pfizer Corporation

We will develop an unmatched number of new products that are recognized worldwide as significantly enhancing health and quality of life.

We will sustain unparalleled vitality in all our product pipelines.

We will attract and retain world-class researchers and product developers who will utilize ever-expanding scientific knowledge to discover life-saving and life-enhancing medicines and health care products.

In the following pages, you will find a tool that can guide you through your organization's vision development process. Directions are provided for each part.

THE VISION DEVELOPMENT PROCESS TOOL

Part One

Part One is about identifying the elements of the desired future state: a vision; a description of where you want your organization to be one, two, three, or five-ten years from now.

Directions: To help you articulate your vision for your organization, answer questions 1-10 by yourself. I have provided you with **guidance statements** for each question; these explain what you need to think about in order to answer the question.

1- What excites you about this organization?

Guidance: The first question addresses a very important aspect which is your motivation as a leader. What motivates you to lead or be part of this organization? You have to address this first and make sure that there are good reasons for your association with this organization. Monetary rewards are not usually enough for a sustained effort on your part. You need to be excited about the organization and it what is stands for, its economic and social purpose, its product and services and your role in making things happen, the recognition you receive and the potential rewards for your time and effort going forward.

2 - What is the purpose of this organization? Provide 5 reasons why you consider it the purpose of the organization

Guidance: An organization must exist for a reason. It is essential to identify the main purpose and mission of your organization. Does it exist to help people find a cure for a health problem or to help people eat healthy foods or to build homes? Why are you in business? Remember making money is an outcome not an end for being in business!

3 - What will the future look like for this organization in your opinion?

Guidance: When you are asked about the vision of your organization? People are interested in an answer that describes what the future will look like, how they fit into it and what it means for the organization, for themselves and for the society within which the organization exists. In your answer to this question, describe what the desired future state of affairs will look like. Be as descriptive as possible using adjectives and metaphors and do not forget to mention what signs will indicate that you have reached the desired future state.

4- What is the urgency behind your vision? What justifies your vision/picture of the future? Why should people rally around it?

Guidance: Many organizational initiatives die at birth because of many factors. One of the main factors is the sense of urgency that everyone sees or does not see for the so-called "desired future state" or "vision". As a leader and manager of an organization, you will need to provide good compelling reasons for changing the current state of affairs. You will also need to communicate this vision and its drivers to your organization and the groups and individuals within it.

5- What core values and beliefs is your vision based on?

Guidance: Core values and beliefs are the elements that will sustain the accomplishments of your vision. Core values and beliefs constitute the supportive culture and fertile ground for the growth of your vision and its accomplishment. Pfizer Corporation's seven core values are:

1.   Contribution

2.   Teamwork

3.   Creativity & Innovation

4.   Integrity

5.   People

6.   Personal Leadership

7.   Quality & Excellence

What are the core values and beliefs of your organization? Do you need to make any changes to them? Will they support your vision for the future? Do the employees believe in them?

Are they adhered to internally?

Are your external stakeholders aware of them?

6- What is a unifying theme for your vision?

Guidance: Having a unifying theme for your vision directs the overall vision statement towards one main common goal such as "delivering on the needs of your customers" or "increasing shareholder return on equity".

7. What key messages will you want this vision to send to:

- The leadership team of this organization?

- The employees/members of this organization?

- Your customers and clients

- Your business partners

- Your competitors

Guidance: A significant part of communicating a vision across an organization is identifying the key messages that all employees need to know and consistently communicate to their peers, customers, suppliers and other businesses.

Key message consistency is vital for the alignment of the vision, strategies, tactical plans and operations.

Develop a communication plan that identifies all parties concerned: leadership team, employees, customers, clients, business partners, suppliers, retailers and competitors. Consider your key messages and what you want to communicate to each one of these constituencies and involve your communications team in the execution of your communication plans. The nature of your execution should be deliberate, focused regular and sustained for maximum effect.

8- List images and metaphors that can more effectively communicate your vision.

Guidance: We all visualize and remember pictures, and metaphors much more than we words. Make use of powerful images and metaphors to help you articulate the attributes of your future organization and its state. Help your listeners see, feel and hear the elements of your envisioned future.

9- What's unique about your organization? What differentiates it from its competition?

Guidance: As you proceed with your vision development, you will need to find some inspiring messages about your organization, your workforce, your products and services. Find out what differentiates this organization, its people and its market position. Build on your successes.

10- Using the answers to the questions above, write a vision statement that captures what the future will look like 3-5 years from now for this organization? When done, meet with your leadership team and deliver your vision speech. Be inspirational; help them see themselves in your vision, use images and metaphors to help them visualize your vision of the future with you. Do not forget to ask for their input and feedback.

Guidance: By answering the above questions, you will be at a good point for securing feedback and validation from your executive team and other main players within your organization. After you have incorporated their feedback where appropriate, you will want to create a vision statement or a speech that helps you communicate the desired future state. Remember that you want to make it as inspiring as possible to your management team, your employees as well as stakeholders.

PART TWO: EXECUTION STEPS

Part Two is about identifying the steps necessary to help you get the organization from where it is now to where it should be based on the vision identified in Part One.

Directions: The following questions should be answered after you have created your vision, validated it and communicated it with your leadership team and business advisors and partners. The following questions address necessary steps your organizations will need to embark on to make the vision a reality. I have provided you with **guidance statements** for each question; these explain what you need to think about in order to answer the question.

In a facilitated session(s) with your leadership team, brainstorm answers to these questions:

1- To realize your vision, what are the major goals you plan for this organization to accomplish? Be as detailed as possible.

Guidance: Since a vision statement articulates the desired future state of affairs, you and your management team will need to identify the steps—strategies and plans—that will get you there. If you looked at the vision and where your organization is today, you will identify a gap between the two. Identifying key strategies to help you bridge this gap is essential for making any progress. You and your team may identify a number of strategies that span internal processes, systems and initiatives and external market-driven objectives you need to achieve.

2- What organizational structures you think will best serve your vision and facilitate its achievement?

Guidance: One of the outcomes of your earlier discussion on strategies is the identification of required resources for the execution on these strategies. These resources include human talent, organizational processes, information technology enablers and the necessary financial resources.

3- What infrastructure and systems will you put in place to achieve these goals?

Guidance: Based on the strategies and resource requirements, you will then need to determine, based on vision priorities, the infrastructure required to support you as you go about implementing these strategies. You will need to devise plans for securing the required infrastructure elements. For example, you may need to increase your sales effectiveness and your customer service delivery. It will become apparent that you need to have an information technology system that enable you to capture, manage and act on the data and what you will know about your customers. You may also need to recruit and hire additional talent to join your forces!

4- How will these organizational structures, strategies and systems fit the current organizational environment?

Guidance: It is imperative to constantly validate the structures and strategies you devise to make sure there is a cultural and operational fit between what you are building today and what has been in place for years. Assess the change readiness of your organization and identify resistance points and address them judiciously. Secure buy-in from all stakeholders as you go about laying the foundation for new structures, systems, and processes.

5- Based on the answers above, write an action plan for achieving these goals and objectives. Ask your leadership team and the leaders throughout the organization to communicate the vision and the action plan to their divisions, departments, teams, employees, customers, business partners and targeted media.

Guidance: The answers to the above four questions constitute a powerful beginning for drafting business strategy documents and plans. The collaboration of your management team and their team members is vital for the success of the ensuing steps. Make sure that alignment of strategies, goals and objectives starts at the vision you have articulated and secured agreement on. Without this top-down alignment, you can end up with many armies; each one fighting a completely different war!

NEXT STEPS:

We offer several options for more in depth and customized work we can do with you and your leadership team.

The San Francisco Leadership Academy offers the following set of options for executive leadership development:

E-Book and Workbook

1. eBook and workbook copies for each individual leadership team member. To download the free workbook, please visit **http://ewotlcco.megaph.com/**

Online Course

This course includes a number of in-depth modules that walk your leadership team through our signature Leadership Development Massive Value Program (MVP) including vision development and explains what it takes to ensure organizational enrollment and adoption. There are a lot of opportunities for self-paced learning, reflection and learning reinforcement through hands-on activities and exercises.

Facebook Leadership Mastermind Group

2. Facebook Mastermind Group: where you get to meet other leaders and share your leadership journey with them, exchange ideas and develop and get feedback from like-minded leadership in a safe environment to practice and get feedback. You can share your vision and other leadership talks via video, audio, written and get feedback from our team of executive coaches. These executive coaches work with you on the content of your leadership talks, and the manner and delivery.

a. You'll also find some resources for download within the Facebook Mastermind Group

EXECUTIVE COACHING VIP DAY

7500.00

Depending on your need an executive coach will work with you to help you develop a compelling vision statement that you can then work on with your leadership team

EXECUTIVE COACHING 6-MONTH PROGRAM

12 1/1 COACHING CALLS (2 PER MONTHS) + 1 VIP DAY

16500.00

3. We also offer executive coaching packages where we pair you up with an executive coach who would work with you 1/1. These packages include working with you on one of our signature talks programs. At the end of these programs you will enhance the confidence you need to deliver your powerful message and vision to your organization and enroll their commitment for it.

LEADERSHIP SUMMIT/RETREAT

150K USD

4. We also offer an offside leadership 2-day retreat/onsite leadership summit where we work with you and a specific number of your leadership team through the leadership journey: key business priorities, vision opportunities and value creation strategies. At the end of the retreat/summit, you and your team have several actionable deliverables:

   a. Business Priorities

   b. Vision for the Future of the Business that everyone can align to

   c. Value Creation Strategies that would improve your revenue streams and your customer loyalty.

PRIVATE LEADERSHIP RETREAT 2.5 DAYS:

75–95K PER PROGRAM DEPENDING ON GROUP SIZE.

This one is focused on high performance leadership communications action learning and feedback program.

This is where we work you and your leadership team on your communications skills and through coaching and actionable learning modules and teams, you build your power toolset and authentic leadership framework.

Overall, these solutions are customizable and can be tailored to fit your organization's needs. Let's start the conversation soon.

Best wishes in your efforts of organizational leadership and visioning.

To download your free vision development workbook, please visit: http://ewotlcco.megaph.com/

You can also order additional copies of the workbook on Amazon.

I am also available via email ash@ashseddeek.com to answer your questions. You can also reach out to me over twitter @ashseddeek or call 9167537432

Reader's Notes

_____

_____

_____

_____

_____

_____

_____

_____

_____

_____

_____

_____

www.ingramcontent.com/pod-product-compliance
Lightning Source LLC
Chambersburg PA
CBHW070751180526
45168CB00004B/1584